BLUES FACES

BLUES FACES
A Portrait of the Blues

PHOTOGRAPHS BY

**Ann Charters
and Samuel Charters**

WITH AN INTRODUCTION AND COMMENTARY BY

Samuel Charters

AN IMAGO MUNDI BOOK

DAVID R. GODINE · PUBLISHER · BOSTON

An *Imago Mundi* book published by
David R. Godine, Publisher, Inc.
P.O. BOX 450, JAFFREY, NEW HAMPSHIRE 03452

Design by Samuel Charters with Scott-Martin Kosofsky and Betsy Sarles.
Typography, composition, and production by Scott-Martin Kosofsky
at The Philidor Company, Cambridge, Massachusetts.
The text typeface is Philidor Bodoni Text.
The display typefaces are Egiziano and Block Berthold.

Library of Congress Cataloging-in-Publication Data:
Charters, Ann.
Blues faces: a portrait of the blues / photographs by Ann Charters and Samuel Charters;
with an introduction and commentary by Samuel Charters.—1st ed.
p. cm.
ISBN: 1-56792-116-7 (hardcover: alk. paper)
1. Blues Musicians—Portraits. I. Charters, Samuel Barclay. II. Title.

ML87 .C57 2000
781.643′092′2—dc21

00-29427

FIRST EDITION
Printed in Hong Kong

Again—

for Frederick Usher

Contents

An Introduction

An Introduction

Sometimes when i look at these photos it's difficult to put myself back into the bare, battered kitchen or the crowded bedroom where Ann and I would sit and listen to someone sing the blues. She would work with her camera, while I worried over the bulky tape recorder we carried with us in the trunk of our small car. It's just as difficult for me to feel the press and grind of the traffic drifting past the street corners where we stood and talked with a singer while his guitar case rested on the sidewalk between us. It's hard to sense the pulse of the band and the loose excitement in the dark and crowded little South Side clubs where the musicians were playing. The world that's there in the photos has changed so much as the years have passed. Some of the buildings are still there, some of the neighborhoods have the same look, even if they've gotten a little shabbier, but most of the country blues singers in the photographs have died, and the bluesmen who were young when she first photographed them don't look the same way now as they did then.

Sometimes as I look at the photographs I have the sense that what they've preserved is another world, and I'm conscious that it's only natural to feel this, since some of the photographs were taken thirty or forty years ago, and so many things have changed in America in the last thirty or forty years. Even in the newer photographs I still have some of this consciousness, since many of them were taken in Africa, or in the bayou country of Louisiana—worlds that are as distant from us as the earlier photos have become with time.

All of the images, all these faces and these neighborhood clubs and empty country roads, went with a way of making music that has almost been lost now, and perhaps that's part of what I feel when I see these faces again. I don't expect to knock on a door in the

St. Louis ghetto and find Daddy Hot Cakes, with his old guitar and two or three friends ready with a harmonica and a washboard to sing me some blues. I know Sleepy John Estes won't be sitting on his chair in front of a neighbor's house on a dirt road outside of Brownsville, waiting in the gleaming sun for someone to come and lead him back over the stumbling dirt path to his cabin. None of this world is left, so I don't expect to see it in these photographs—but somehow it's there.

When I first went to the South to look for the older kinds of black music, it was jazz that I was trying to find—the jazz of the old pioneer musicians in New Orleans. It was 1950, and there was still music everywhere in the city. I went to every music funeral I could find, I tried to talk to every musician I'd ever heard about, and I went to every neighborhood bar that had a little band. I took my first photographs with a cheap camera at a gray, rainy funeral with the Eureka Brass Band, and despite the crudeness of the images they still give me the feeling of excited disbelief that I had found so much still there to hear and to see and to experience. I was able to buy a clumsy—and heavy—Pentron tape recorder in 1953, and I began recording small sessions in the spring of the next year. I never was able to buy a better camera, but for the next few years I went on taking photographs of the musicians I was recording or to illustrate the books I was writing.

I had already found the country blues, and one of the first sessions I did in New Orleans in that spring of 1954 was with a street evangelist named Blind Dave Ross, who told me that I might still find Blind Willie Johnson alive in Texas. Then a month or so later I drove to Mobile to look for the legendary country skiffle group, the Mobile Strugglers; I spent an afternoon with them, recording in a house at the edge of Mobile's black section. Nearly all of those first blues recordings were done in peo-

Albert Warner of the Eureka Brass Band, playing for a funeral. New Orleans, 1950.

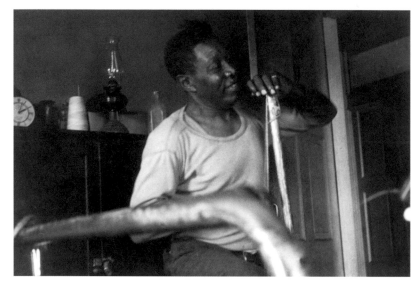

Will Shade of the Memphis Jug Band, playing a washtub bass. Memphis, 1956.

ple's front rooms or kitchens, and I was trying to do everything. I had to encourage the singer, sometimes help tune the guitar, keep track of the songs, and operate the tape recorder.

I had to hold the microphone in one hand to keep the singers from leaning too close and distorting the sound on the tape. At the same time I tried to take pictures. The pictures had to wait until last, and when we'd finished recording both the singer and I were usually too tired to do anything else.

In the summer of 1958 I went to Andros Island in the Bahamas to document the music of the black communities of sponge fishermen who lived in a thin scattering of villages along the island's west coast. A young woman named Ann Danberg, whom I'd met in a music class at the University of California in Berkeley, went on the trip with me. Even though she was using an old camera she'd bought for $10 just before she left Berkeley, the photographs she did on Andros caught the mood and the atmosphere of the music so well that they were used for the album covers of the LPs that Folkways produced of the music we'd recorded. We were married the next spring, and for almost ten years it was Ann's photographs that were used for most of the books and articles and albums covers. By this time she had bought a used Rolleiflex, which she still prefers for portraits, but there were also a series of 35mm cameras before she finally decided on a Nikon for her second camera.

As I look back over the portraits I can see two different kinds of images, and they reflect the different worlds of the blues that we were working in during these years. In the 1950s and the 1960s most of the musicians were country blues singers, and they sit on old chairs in their kitchens under the light of a glaring bulb, or they're in the back yard of a weathered frame house with—usually just out of sight of the camera—dozens of neighbors standing around in the hot sun, wondering what was going on. In the middle of the 1960s, however, the background for many of the photographs had changed. Instead of front rooms or kitchens, we were using recording studios. The Chicago blues, with its amplified guitars and drums and pianos and saxophones, was too complicated to record with a portable tape machine and a hand-held microphone.

The years of recording and photographing in the South were spent in small towns or in the ghettos of cities like Memphis or St. Louis, and the way of life the photographs reflect was stifled in isolation and poverty. There were often more difficulties working there than we experienced later in the much more violent sections of South Side Chicago. In the South the problems came from the racial tensions that dominated the countryside during this period. Most of the recording and research trips were made between 1956 and 1972, and it was during these years that the South burst into open violence around the voter registration drives, the attempts of the Freedom Riders to integrate public facilities, and the bus boycott in Selma, Alabama. In every restaurant where we stopped there was a list of telephone numbers taped up by the cash register for the employees to call if any of the Freedom Riders came through in their busses and tried to get something to eat. The numbers were for the local sheriff, the state police, the National Guard, and the fire department.

On one of the trips we were driving to New Orleans from New York in an old Volkswagen with New York license plates. A few days after the bodies of Chaney, Werner, and Goodman, who had been working for the Voter Registration Drive, were found in Mississippi, we passed through Birmingham, and we stopped long enough for Ann to photograph a row of shacks in the city's ramshackle black ghetto. Even though the buildings were dilapidated and almost uninhabitable there was a "For Rent" sign on the one closest to the street where we were passing. She was using the Rolleiflex, which needs some time to compose the image in the view-finder, but she was only intending to shoot one roll of film, which is just twelve exposures.

She had taken no more than three or four exposures when another car passed ours, driven by a white woman whose car had Alabama license plates. She slowed down enough to

The Mobile Strugglers: from left, Moochie Reeves, Ollie Crenshaw, and Tyler Jackson. Mobile 1954.

On a hot, muggy night in the summer of 1952 I was passing through Mobile, Alabama, on a Greyhound bus. As it passed an empty store front downtown I heard music, and through the window I saw a country skiffle band playing in front of the store. There were two guitar players, a washtub bass player, and another man who was playing a kazoo and a washboard. The piece they were playing was a kind of music I'd thought was lost forever. By the time the bus pulled off the street two blocks later to let me off and I ran back to the store front, sweating in my Army uniform, they'd gone. I couldn't find them again, despite hours looking up and down the streets of Mobile's small business section.

I had to wait until I was discharged from the Army to look for them again, and in the spring of 1954 I drove over from New Orleans with my wife then, and a friend in his small coupe. The tape recorder was packed with our suitcases in the trunk of the car. Despite the Mobile police, who kept insisting that we get out of what they thought was a dangerous neighborhood, we managed to find somebody about midnight who knew where the band was, and we arranged to record them the next day.

The next morning I had to get the washtub player out of jail and buy him a new washtub, since the police had picked him up for being drunk and disorderly the night before and his instrument had gotten lost in the confusion. We also had to do without the washboard player, who had moved to Houston, but once we all had a little to drink and they started playing it didn't really matter. It turned out that they lived in the country, outside of Selma, and they didn't know anybody in the rundown neighborhood where they were waiting for me. I had to find someplace to plug in the tape recorder. A crowd had gathered, and someone suggested that we could use a house close to where they'd parked their truck.

Once inside the living room we had to push the furniture around, and the only thing I could find to hold the microphone was an ironing board, but despite the heat and the crowd in the little space they recorded some intensely beautiful blues and medicine show songs. Then the door of the house opened and two or three new people came in, looking at us

wide-eyed. It was their house. I had assumed that the people who had led us up to the porch lived there, but they were only neighbors who knew the owners were out, and they hoped they wouldn't mind. With much embarrassment we managed to get everybody outside and the furniture moved back and the woman of the house, who was beginning to laugh by this time, helped me fold up the ironing board. It was my introduction to recording the country blues.

stare angrily at us, then drove on, and I could see her stop and use a telephone in a booth on the corner fifty feet ahead. Before Ann could get back in the car and put her camera away our car was hemmed in by two Army trucks filled with uniformed soldiers. A highway patrol car nudged in beside us and the officer inside gestured emphatically for us to begin driving. The Army trucks escorted us to the city limits, and we were so frightened that we drove to New Orleans without stopping for anything except gas, pushing the tired and hot little car as fast as it would go.

Most of the questioning we had to put up with from local sheriffs and police officers, and the angry exchanges we had with people in small towns who didn't want us to talk to their "niggras," doesn't show in the photos, although sometimes the tension was reflected in the faces of the people Ann was photographing. In Chicago, on the crumbling streets of the South Side ghetto, it was the poverty and the violence that made it difficult to stay close to the musicians. It was usually all right to go into the clubs and listen to the bands, though some of the clubs in the worst sections of the ghetto were bossed by the gangs that filled the neighborhood, and it wasn't safe to walk out into the dark streets for more than a block from the door of the club. I usually carried record album jackets with me, so it would be clear that I wasn't looking for local sex, and I wasn't a plain-clothes policeman.

One night in the battered southern tip of the city, close to the Indiana line, in a gritty neighborhood where the steel mills filled the air with bellowing sounds and a coughing pall of smoke, I followed Mighty Joe Young's band into a half-lit club so I could listen to some of his new pieces for a recording session a few days later. I had a handful of album covers and I put them out on the table I found close to the bandstand. Nobody said anything to me, but I could see some heads turning at a table on the other side of the dance floor, where three or four of the neighborhood bloods were studying me. After a pause long enough so I'd know they didn't think I really was worth worrying about, a thin, wiry man in his twenties, with a Stetson hat and a handkerchief knotted around his neck, sauntered to the table where I was sitting. He picked up the album jackets, looked at them one by one, then stared at me questioningly. I said as clearly as I could over the noise of the band, "I make records," and after a moment he put them back on the table and walked away. Nobody else bothered me while I was in the club.

The Chicago police, unlike the southern sheriffs, didn't want any trouble in their districts, and sometimes Ann and I would come out of a club and find that a police car was parked across the street, and it had obviously been there for an hour or so, making sure nothing happened while we were inside. The police carefully didn't look our way, but on some of the snowy nights when it had gotten very late it was reassuring to see them there.

Pepper's Lounge, Muddy Water's "home club." Chicago, 1966.

Samuel Charters in the studio with Muddy Waters and Otis Spann.

In 1964 Muddy Waters brought his band into New York for a concert in Carnegie Hall, and they were so poorly paid that they didn't have enough money to get back to Chicago. I set up a recording session for Prestige Records, the company I was with at the time, and paid them an advance of $750 to take care of travel expenses. I couldn't use Muddy's name, since he was under contract to Chess Records, and two members of the band, Otis Spann, the pianist, and Jimmy Cotton, the harmonica player, had to do the singing. It was their first appearance on LP, and they were so pleased to be recording that they mostly danced during the playbacks. It was still Muddy's session, though, and we had to turn to him to get anything decided.

Otis Spann and James Cotton with the Muddy Waters band, recording in New York, 1964.

MANY OF THE PORTRAITS were taken for the book *The Poetry of the Blues*, published in 1963, and Ann had to decide how she wanted to photograph the singers. She didn't want to create the kind of sociological portraits that had been so important in the 1930s and 1940s. She didn't want to turn the musicians into something like representatives of a poor underclass. She thought of them simply as artists, and this was what she tried to bring out in the portraits. Sometimes she worked in the clubs, but except for nights when we brought lights into places like Theresa's in Chicago so she could photograph Junior Wells and Buddy Guy in color it was usually too dark to capture much more than the mood of the musicians and the crowd.

In June 1967, a year after Ann had finished her Ph.D. in American Literature at Columbia University, she began teaching at Brooklyn Community College, and our first daughter was born. It was almost impossible for her to follow me on the recording trips. This meant I had to go back to taking my own photographs. I made several trips back to the United States in the 1970s, recording Cajun music in Louisiana, and doing a series of recordings for the series of albums and the book *The Legacy of the Blues*. I couldn't use Ann's Rolleiflex—in a number of tries I was never even able to focus it—but I borrowed her Nikon. Many of the photographs I took in the Mississippi delta blues country were used to illustrate the book *Robert Johnson* in 1973.

When I traveled to Africa in the mid 1970s I also had a camera, and I used it for the album covers for a series of recordings and for the book *The Roots of the Blues*. The camera wasn't always welcome out in the African countryside. In Ghana if I came into a village street with a camera around my neck the women who were sitting with small piles of fruit and roots to sell would scatter with a shout, and in a moment the little dirt street would be deserted. Their bright robes and high voices always gave me the feeling that I had surprised a flock of beautiful, shy birds.

As I said, when I look again at some of these images it's difficult for me to believe that it all happened—that these men and women stood in the hot sun outside their doorways in a St. Louis ghetto street to let us take their picture. That they waited patiently on a front porch on a dirt road outside of Brownsville, Tennessee for Ann to focus her stubborn Rolleiflex, or that they let us sit in their kitchens in Memphis, or Spartanburg, or brought us with them to the rundown clubs in Louisiana or Chicago's South Side where they played—that they let us see their lives. If some of this is there in the photographs, if for a moment the black and white image catches some suggestion of the careful dignity or sudden, casual cheerfulness that these singers brought to their lives, then it is some small repayment for all that they gave us.

—SAMUEL CHARTERS

A Portrait of the Blues

Thinking of Home

Thinking of Home

SOME AFRICAN GRIOTS

In FEBRUARY 1974, a run-down school bus that was being used to bring people back and forth from the airport stopped behind a large, dimly lit building on a dark street in Banjul, the small, isolated capital of The Gambia. There was a half-obliterated sign painted on the wall saying that it was a hotel. The driver stopped long enough for me to pull my bags out of the makeshift luggage compartment, then he rattled off into the darkness. One of the canvas shoulder bags was stuffed with clothes and guide books, and the other—the larger one—was filled with a tape recorder, microphones, blank tapes, a transformer, and an assortment of plugs so that I could use whatever electrical current I might find along the west coast of Africa.

It wasn't a coincidence that it was 1974. I'd done my first documentary recordings of New Orleans jazz musicians and blues singers in 1954, and the trip to Africa was my own private commemoration of the twenty years of recording that had passed since then. It also wasn't a coincidence that I was in The Gambia. The research I had been doing suggested that I might find some trace of the backgrounds of the blues in The Gambia, a small, English speaking enclave in the center of one of the cultural areas that had contributed so many of the vivid threads that make up the cultural weave in the United States. I wasn't thinking of all these things as I stood on the shadowy street and listened to the bus clatter away, but it was part of the background that kept me coming back to Africa over the next two years, and finally took shape in the book *The Roots of the Blues.*

The fact that I was looking mostly in Africa for blues roots determined many of the places I traveled and the musicians I recorded. I wanted to see if there were any traces of the blues in the songs of the West African griots, the tribal instrumentalists who also play stringed instruments and create the songs and music for their own villages. The music of West Africa and the American South have developed in such different ways since they separated two hundred years ago that it was often hard to trace the relationships between the two, but sometimes I was startled at how similar they still are, despite all that has happened to both cultures.

As I listened to the singers I met in the African villages, I often had the feeling that I'd heard echoes of the way they shaped their voices and the ways they developed rhythms out in the countryside in Alabama and Tennessee. I was certain that if a Mississippi blues singer and a Mandingo griot could sing for each other, in a moment they would begin to take on each other's vocal inflections and subtle phrases.

West Africa is sweeping into the 20th Century, but many of the new nations, whatever else they're struggling to achieve, have made serious efforts to preserve some of their older cultures. The best known griots often have some kind of government subsidy, and there still are hours of traditional music on the national radio. Two of the most important Mandingo griots in The Gambia lived in small compounds outside of Banjul. Each of them was the center of a complicated extended family, with their wives and children living in separate houses in the compounds—which were dusty plots of earth surrounded by high fences constructed out of rusting corrugated iron, with three or four stucco buildings that had windows and doors open to the compound yard and its piles of refuse, chickens, children, and goats.

The griot Jali Nyama Suso played the *kora,* a stringed lyre with two banks of plastic strings stretched over a dried calabash covered with a goat skin. He performed on the national radio service once a week, and since he was playing regularly he knew dozens of songs. In the villages the griot's main job is to sing at christenings and name day ceremonies, where they perform long, laudatory narratives celebrating the surname of the family who is paying them to sing. A griot like Jali Nyama not only knows the important historical narratives, he also has to know the backgrounds of all the families in the village.

*Mandingo griot
Jali Nyama Suso.
The Gambia, 1974.*

The other griot, Alhaji Fabala Kanuteh, played a small *balafon,* the traditional wooden keyed instrument of the Mandingo griots, which developed into the marimba and the vibraphone in the western hemisphere. He was one of the two official griots appointed to the president of The Gambia, and he performed many of the classic long narratives. As he told me in the small, cramped room where he recorded for me, "I can tell you the history of everything. Africa, India, China, everything. But you must come when you have time to listen."

WHAT THESE GRIOTS SANG FOR ME was so compelling in its concentration and artistry that even without understanding the words of the songs I sat motionless and spellbound with the small groups that gathered to listen in the small rooms in the littered compounds, with bright flowered curtains blowing in the doorways and the children and the chickens scrabbling over bits of garbage in the heaps near the gate. The other people listening had heard the songs many times before, but they were still totally absorbed, and the songs always changed so there were new things every time the griots sang them. At the end of a piece there would be a murmur of approval, and the listeners who were the most moved would reach in their pockets for the traditional "shilling" to give the singer as thanks.

When later I had people help me with translations of the songs, I found a rich panorama of history unfolding for me. I felt then that a long narrative that Alhaji Fabala Kanuteh sang for me was one of the most important things I'd ever recorded. I had asked him to tell me about the first meeting with the Europeans and the first sale of slaves. He tapped the wooden keys of the *balafon* and looked thoughtful: "It is a hard song to do and it goes on for a day and a half."

In the song he described the first encounter between the Portuguese and the people living along the coast, and the first sale of slaves to people he called the "Hollanders." With the spare, leaf-dry sound of the *balafon* tapping out a little rhythmic figure behind his voice and filling in with an occasional flourish when his voice was tired, he sang the song for me, ending his story with the little he knew of what had happened to the people later.

. . . When the Europeans came,

when they brought their ship from Portugal,

the ship used to start its journey from Banjul,

then it went to Sanemunko Joyo to collect slaves there

in the presence of King Seneke Jammeh, and Mansa Demba Sanko,

and Samkala Marong and Wali Mandeba and Jata Sela.

Anyone who had slaves, they collected them all together

and took them to the places called Aladabara and Jufure

to sell them to the Portuguese.

Then the Portuguese put them in their ship

and left there and went to Jang Jang Bure.

When they arrived there they went

right to the slave house to collect the slaves there,

and take them to the Hollanders.

Then the Hollanders collected them and sent them to America.

It is because of this that slaves are plenty in America.

They call them American Negroes.

Alhaji Fabala Kanuteh.
Banjul, 1974.

Alhaji Amara Sahone

When R&B artist Johnny Otis heard recordings of Alhaji Samara Sahone he said that this came closest to the blues of anything he had heard in traditional African music. Sahone was a member of the Serehule tribe, but he lived in the same settlement as Mandingo griot Jali Nyama Suso. He played an instrument called the *konting*, which comes from Mali. It is almost twice as large as the *halam*, the instrument played by the Wollof griot Alhaji Sait Camara, but has only four strings. The inner two strings are fretted, and the outer two are tied to the neck of the instrument as drones. The playing style is harder and more rhythmic than the music of the *halam*, with some of the rolling feel of Kentucky banjo playing. By the time the first blues recording were made, most of the rural African-American musicians had turned from the banjo to the guitar, but the playing of an older artist like Gus Cannon may reflect some of these earlier techniques.

Sahone was a tall, still man, with the characteristic Serehule facial markings, and he sang the traditional narratives in a dark, skillfully modulated vocal style. The Serehule people are thought of as great travelers, and they are held in great respect for their energy and their business acumen. As the title "Alhaji" indicates, Sahone had made the "haj," the journey to the holy shrine at Mecca for observant Muslims, and he had traveled throughout much of Africa. Also, the world, even for African village musicians, has grown steadily smaller. Although it isn't visible in the photograph, his *konting* was fitted with an electric pickup, and he had recently returned from playing a concert at a culture festival in Paris.

Alhaji Amara Sahone.
Banjul, 1974.

Alhaji Sait Camara

The Gambia is surrounded on three sides by Senegal, and many Wollofs, who belong to the dominant tribe of this area of Senegal, also live in Banjul. The Wollof singers play a different instrument, a small ancestor of the banjo called the *halam*. It's constructed out of a dried gourd and a stick, with the head covered with goatskin. There is a painting of a slave dance in the United States from the 18th century and one of the musicians has a crude *halam*. It is a five-string instrument with all the characteristics of the American folk banjo, and even with its light, gentle tone I could hear all of the techniques that had come to the United States with the instrument.

Sait Camara was a Wollof griot, or *halamkat*, as griots are usually called in Wollof. *Kat* means someone who plays an instrument. He was a quiet, unassuming artist, with a delicate touch on his instrument. The first song he recorded—so there would be no uncertainty about his political attitudes—was a praise song to the president of The Gambia.

Alhaji Sait Camara.
Banjul, 1974.

Two Fula jelefos, *as griots are titled in the Fula language, Baba Jale Sowe with the calabash, and Satala Kurubally with the one-string fiddle called the* riti. *The Gambia, 1974.*

A village brass band, Ghana, 1974

A griot's hands.
Jali Nyama Suso

Goin' Up The Country

Goin' Up The Country

THE COUNTRY BLUES

THE BEGINNINGS OF THE BLUES will probably always be lost, but as far as the early singers could remember the blues grew out of field hollers and work gang chants in the lonely rows of weathered shacks along the muddy dirt roads in the Mississippi delta around the end of the 19th century. The first blues recordings in the 1920s were a vaudeville version of the earthy blues songs that singers like Ma Rainey had heard in the delta towns before World War I, but as early as 1923 and 1924 small "race" labels were already recording the country blues artists who had created their own way of playing out in the isolated countryside.

The companies mostly sold the records by mail order through advertisements in the black newspapers like *The Chicago Defender* that were beginning to spread through the South. Most little crossroads stores also had their stacks of records, and in the "Five and Dime" stores in the small towns there was also a counter of records that was filled with new releases every week. When the companies started sending recording teams to the South to look for new songs to release they used local music store owners to find the singers for them, and for the next fifteen years—until World War II and the Musicians' Union recording ban—there was a steady stream of recordings that caught some of the inexhaustible variety and individual creativity of the country blues.

In the 1950s and 1960s, even though a lot of the excitement drifted north with the younger musicians like Muddy Waters and Howling Wolf who followed the great wave of black migration to cities like Chicago and Detroit, there was still blues out in the country. The singers were still living in small towns or along back country roads, or in cities like Memphis or St. Louis, where many of them had moved when they couldn't take any more of the poorly paid field work and the harsh discrimination that faced them out on the cotton farms. The regional styles of the blues—Mississippi's bottleneck, the Carolinas' finger picking, the high, wailing sound of the Texas blues, the jug bands of Memphis—were still there, giving the new kinds of blues a vital background and perspective.

Most of the country musicians still played by themselves, or they added another musician to play bass or harmonica. Some of them didn't even go to the trouble of buying an electric guitar. When I wanted to record bluesmen like Furry Lewis or Lightning Hopkins in the 1950s I had to go down to a local pawn shop and rent them a guitar. A lot of the singers didn't have much chance to play in public, and sometimes their friends almost didn't believe them when they talked about their recording careers ". . . in them old days." What kept them singing their old songs was a stubborn pride in what they'd done, and an equally stubborn belief that the blues was something worth holding on to. When Furry Lewis walked out to the car to go with me for his first session in a recording studio in thirty years, he stopped in the middle of the street in his north Memphis neighborhood, held up the guitar I'd just rented, and called out to anybody who might be listening behind their windows, "Good-bye, you all, I'm going to go do some recording!"

Daddy Hot Cakes

"Daddy Hot Cakes," whose name was George Montgomery, was born in Georgia, but after years of wandering with circuses or small shows—often as a fire eater—he settled down in St. Louis, and during the 1940s and 1950s he made his living sitting in the back row of seats in the street cars—in the segregated section—performing his blues with a washboard player or somebody who played a harmonica. He rode the street cars all day, passing a hat around to collect enough money to live on. When I met him in 1961, St. Louis had changed, and he couldn't play on the street cars anymore. Instead, he was working as a janitor and watchman. All of his blues were spontaneously improvised, and on the afternoons when we recorded in his small room in a dark tenement I never had any idea what kind of song he would decide to do next. If I had to stop him—sometimes he couldn't wait for the tape machine to be turned on—he usually would go on with the same general idea for his blues, but there would be a new melody and a new story that he worked into the verses.

The themes of his blues were as unpredictable as his music. When he listened back to one of the songs he decided it was called "Please Don't Sass My Grandmother." Another one had verses that turned into "I Ride My Horses Everywhere," and he called another "Hawaiian Dream Blues." When I asked him where the songs came from he smiled and casually explained, "I got remembrance of things."

"Daddy Hot Cakes."
St. Louis, 1961.

Memphis Willie B.

Willie Boerum—"Memphis Willie B."—hadn't had a chance to record his own blues when he first started singing in the Depression years, and he wasn't going to miss his opportunity when it came around again. Will Shade of the Memphis Jug Band had improvised an audition for me in the noisy room of an old frame building behind Beale Street where he was living in 1961, and the only person there who didn't drink too much wine and get involved in a chaotic jam session was a younger bluesman I'd never met before named Willie Boerum. He'd brought a cheap guitar with him, and he sang for me outside where it was quiet enough to hear his intense voice and strong accompaniment style. He had a little business repairing radios and television sets, so he wasn't playing often, and when we went into the studio to record his first album for the Prestige/Bluesville series I had to rent a new guitar for him. The metal strings cut into his fingers, and he was bleeding by the time we got to his last blues, but he wouldn't stop playing. He just kept saying that it didn't hurt and it didn't bother him, and was there any other song I'd like him to sing.

Willie Boerum,
"Memphis Willie B."
Memphis, 1961.

Furry Lewis

Furry was one of the blues legends of the 1920s, and his bottleneck version of "John Henry" inspired hundreds of much younger players in the 1960s. He was a slight, wry, thoughtful man who had lost a leg when he was hopping freight cars as a boy. Fitted with an artificial limb, he walked with a pronounced limp. Despite his handicap, when I found him in Memphis in 1959 he had been working for almost thirty years sweeping the gutters in the neighborhood around Beale Street for the City Maintenance Department. He grew up playing the guitar on some of the same streets, and he knew almost every guitar tuning and picking style that had come up to Memphis from northern Mississippi.

Later the same year, for a recording that was released on Folkways Records, I rented a guitar for him from a Beale Street pawn shop and set up the tape recorder in the shabby furnished room he was renting on a back street in North Memphis. His neighbors crowded in the hallway to listen through the open doorway and the session turned into a noisy party. Two years later, when Prestige Records sent me to record him again, I decided to use the Sun Recording Studios, where Elvis Presley, Johnny Cash, and Jerry Lee Lewis had gotten their start. The recording engineer was Elvis's lead guitarist, Scotty Moore, and I spent most of the day listening to them talk over guitar tunings. Every time Furry started a new song Scotty would ask over the studio talkback, "What you doing with that guitar now?" and he would walk into the studio to find out how Furry was playing. Scotty occasionally mentioned Elvis Presley when he was talking to Furry, but as far as I could tell Furry had never heard of him.

Furry Lewis.
Memphis, 1962.

I was born in the country . . .

Sleepy John Estes

Winfield Lane is a rutted, dusty dirt lane that crosses a stretch of nondescript fields outside of Brownsville, Tennessee. To get to the lane in the summer of 1962 you went through the center of town, past its rundown courthouse square and its streets lined with small town businesses and ordinary frame houses behind trimmed lawns and painted fences. It was like a postcard view of what a small town in western Tennessee should look like. It wasn't much different from a hundred others in the hilly, wooded countryside outside of Memphis, where the dried leaves lay thick and brown along the country fences in the autumn, and the haze seemed to close the horizon in around the edge of town in the summer.

Brownsville, though, was different for us, since in a way we already knew something about it. The great country blues singer Sleepy John Estes had sung about the town and some of the people who lived in it on the recordings he'd made in the '20s and '30s. In his high, quavering voice, John had sung about Brownsville's sheriff, two of its lawyers, about a local mortician, Al Rawls, and a liquor store owner named Peter Albert. He had even sung about the man who repaired his car, Vassie Williams, who lived in the nearby town of Durhamville.

In one of his first blues he described how to get to Brownsville from Memphis:

Now I'm going to Brownsville, take that right hand road . . .

and in another song he described where he was living:

I was raised in Lawdry County, you know I was schooled on
Winfield Lane.

But the Chicago blues singer Big Bill Broonzy had written about John in his informal auto-biography, and he had said that John was dead. Since he sounded so sure about what he was saying we hadn't taken the right hand road out of Memphis to Brownsville to find out what had happened to Sleepy John Estes, even though it was John, of all the country blues

Overleaf: *Sleepy John Estes. Brownsville, 1962.*

singers, who moved Ann the most deeply. Then in 1962 a young film maker named David Blumenthal, who was documenting the civil rights struggle in Tennessee, found John in Brownsville. He was still living in Lawdry Country, out on Winfield Lane.

It was hot under the summer sun, and the car stirred up a column of dust behind us as we drove out to look for John's cabin. A neighbor, Philip Mieux, was going to take us to him. In the years since he'd made his records he'd become blind, and was living in poverty with a wife and small children. There was a scattering of abandoned shacks in the burnt fields beside the uneven road, but one of them, despite its gaping walls and open door, still seemed to have people living in it. A vine had straggled up the tar paper sides of the sagging building, and a single flower dangled in front of the door. There was a scattering of broken chairs and chipped porcelain plates on the trampled earth in front of the shack, and a pan of something that looked like food had been left out for the heat and the flies. It was the cabin where John was living with his family.

A hundred yards further we came to the Mieux house, a weather-beaten wooden building with a long front porch. In front of it a spindly man in a faded striped shirt and dirty chino trousers was sitting in a battered kitchen chair in the sun, waiting for us. He was wearing a stained straw hat, but it was pushed back from his forehead and I could see that he was bald. His skin was drawn tightly over the bones of his cheeks and jaw, and even from across the yard we could see a line of white film around his closed eyes. A serviceable, but much-handled guitar was across his lap, and to change the pitch when he sang, a pencil had been tied across the guitar neck with a piece of string. The man sitting in the chair was John Estes.

THE NEIGHBOR'S DESCRIPTION of what had happened to John was as simple and as obvious as the sunlight that pressed its heavy weight down on us as we stood around his chair. The help he received from the state welfare office was too little to do much more than pay the rent on the half-ruined shack and buy some food for the children. His wife wasn't able to take any kind of job. When he had one of his children lead him into town to shop, Mieux

Sleepy John Estes's wife, 1962.

thought that sometimes the store owners took advantage of his blindness to cheat him out of his change. Now John hoped that someone would help him to start singing again. It was the only way he could think of to get out of his poverty. We spent the day with him recording and filming, and Ann photographed John and his wife and their children. When we left we paid him what we could and drove back to our motel in town, so upset with what we had experienced that it was hours before we could talk about it with each other.

As impossible as it seemed that day, however, John did get out of the shack on Winfield Lane. Thanks primarily to Bob Koester, owner of Delmark Records, a small company that specializes in the blues, he did have a second career. Koester came down from Chicago, bought him some "slack britches" and a better guitar, released a new album on Delmark and presented John's music to the enthusiastic young audience that was growing up with the blues revival. There were tours to Europe, John was able to buy a little house in Brownsville, and in 1964, only two years after we'd first seen him in front of Philip Mieux's house on Winfield Lane, I walked into a room in one of the houses where the artists were staying for the Newport Folk Festival and there was a stylishly dressed John Estes sitting quietly on a cot. He was in a tie, suit coat, and a new straw hat, and he was waiting for one of musicians who had recorded with him thirty years before to come and lead him to the stage so he could sing his old blues for a new audience that he had never seen.

Bukka White

Booker T. Washington "Bukka" White was another of the great creative blues artists of the 1930s who was found still living in the South during the blues revival. His "Fixin' To Die Blues" was recorded by Bob Dylan on his first album, and Country Joe and the Fish used the title for their anti-Vietnam war song "I-Feel-Like-I'm-Fixin-To-Die-Rag." He spent most of the '30s in Parchman Prison Farm, where he'd been sent for murder, but when he was released in 1940 he recorded twelve classic blues, some of them involved with his prison experiences. One of the songs was called "Aberdeen Mississippi Blues":

> *Aberdeen is my home, but the mens don't want me around . . .*

Mississippi John Hurt had also recorded a blues about his home town, Avalon, Mississippi, and after a letter to Avalon led to his rediscovery a young guitarist named John Fahey sent a letter to "Booker T. Washington White (Old Blues Singer), c/o General Delivery, Aberdeen." The South is still a countryside of small towns and long family memories, and a relative in Mississippi forwarded the letter to Bukka in Memphis.

When he agreed to an afternoon photo session in 1974 he wanted to be photographed in his "office," three or four worn chairs he had set up on the sidewalk beside an empty building a few blocks from his apartment. When he wasn't out of town on a tour he walked to his "office" in the afternoon. Friends would usually show up, and they'd talk away the rest of the day.

Bukka White.
Memphis, 1974.

Baby Tate

In Spartanburg, South Carolina, in the late spring of 1962, we filmed the veteran blues singer Baby Tate in his ramshackle board house on a dirt street in one of Spartanburg's black neighborhoods. By the middle of the afternoon we had finished with the filming, but we wanted to do some additional recording. I had already produced an album with Baby the year before for the Prestige Bluesville series, but I wanted to get more of his music down while we were there.

We were sitting in his bare front room, with his wife and young son in the kitchen at the end of a short hallway so the baby's noise wouldn't be picked up on the tape. As usual I was holding the microphone in an outstretched hand, ready to shift it down toward the guitar when he played a solo. Ann was sitting across the room with a notebook, keeping track of what we were recording. I looked out the window that opened on the back yard and suddenly I saw a large, heavy-set white man in a police uniform coming toward the back door. He had a pistol in his hand. At the same moment Ann saw another officer coming toward the front door, also carrying a pistol.

The doors were banged open—they weren't locked—and the two policemen crowded into the small room, weapons drawn. One of them seemed to be the sheriff, the other his deputy. The sheriff stared at us—at the black man from his town who had a white couple in his living room, a young white couple with out-of-state license plates on their dusty car.

"We heard you were selling moonshine in here," he said after a long silence. He was still staring at us. The tape recorder and boxes of tape were scattered across the floor, I was holding a microphone, and Baby was holding his guitar. There wasn't anything to drink in the room. Obviously disappointed but not sure what to do next, the two officers decided to search the house, still pretending to look for illegal corn whiskey. We sat without moving. I still can remember that it was a bright, hot day, and the sun was fresh and yellow on the dirt street outside the window, and from where I was sitting I could see the sunflowers Baby was growing in a straggling little garden against his fence.

After heavy clumping in the other rooms, and some questioning of Baby's wife, the two of them came back in the room. Finally they put their pistols back in their holsters, but they still didn't say anything. Finally, with a nod from the sheriff, the deputy started toward the door. As they were leaving, the sheriff turned back to me and said with a terse smile, "They sure got rhythm, don't they."

A half hour later Ann photographed the family in front of the house. Baby was standing at the bottom of the wooden steps, and his wife was on the porch behind him, holding their son in her arms. Baby was trying to look confident, with his guitar across his chest and a cigar clenched in his teeth, but clearly something was worrying him. He looked nervous. On the porch his wife's worry was more obvious, and the child sensed the mood and started to cry. At a glance the image might suggest the casual independence of the wandering bluesman and the unhappiness of the woman who is left behind with a child in her arms, but what both of them knew was that as soon as Ann and I had driven away, the sheriff and his deputy would be back.

Above: *Baby Tate. Spartanburg, 1962.*

Overleaf: *Baby Tate with his family. Spartanburg, 1962.*

J. D. Short

J. D. Short had left Mississippi in the 1920s and gone to work in a factory in St. Louis, so his way of playing and singing stayed with him only as a memory from his old life, and nothing about his blues ever really changed. When I met him in the early 1960s he still played occasionally, though he was probably better known around his neighborhood for his harmonica style. His cousin, the blues singer Big Joe Williams, would come into town for a few months and they'd play in the neighborhood clubs together, then Big Joe would go off on tour or up to Chicago to see friends, and J. D. would put his guitar away until Joe's next visit. He'd been injured while he was in training for military service in World War II, and he had a small pension that helped him get by in a little upstairs corner apartment on Delmark Avenue in the St. Louis ghetto. He had a way of singing with a broad vibrato that made his jaw tremble, and when he did his first recordings in the 1920s he was called "Jelly Jaw Short" on the record label.

J. D. was a gentle, calm man who had thought a lot about what he was singing and why he was singing it. When I asked him about what makes a good blues song, he answered, "What I think about that makes the blues really good is when a fellow writes a blues and then writes it with a feeling, with great harmony, and there's so many true words in the blues, of things that have happened to so many people, and that's why it makes the feeling in the blues."

J. D. Short.
St. Louis, 1961.

Pink Anderson

Pink Anderson was a gangling, easy-going man who had spent most of his life traveling with medicine shows singing blues, doing comedy routines, sometimes even trying a little eccentric dancing—whatever it took to sell the medicine. He traveled for years with a partner named Simmie Dooley, and he did his first recording with Simmie in the 1920s. When I first met Pink in 1961, in his small frame house not far from Baby Tate's house in Spartanburg, Simmie had died, and the medicine shows had stopped going out in the spring, and Pink spent his time playing cards, occasionally walking over to talk to Baby, and trying to teach his son how to play the guitar.

In the afternoons we spent working together in his front room I tried to record all the songs he could think of. The moonshine we were drinking was so coarse that we had to strain it through a piece of cloth to get the bits of stick and small stones out of it, but what we had, finally, was a portrait of a southern rural songster. Pink knew ballads, hymns, children's songs, and all the comedy songs he'd performed when he was out with the shows. He also performed a lot of blues, but they were only a part of the music he had in his head and his fingers. When all the material came out on the Bluesville series we needed three albums to include all the sides of Pink's musical personality.

When Ann and I came back to film him in 1962 he was still trying to show his son how to make chords on the guitar, and they went out in the back yard for a session together. By the time they'd finished, the whole neighborhood was standing out of range of Ann's camera listening to them, but Pink, as a veteran performer, didn't show any sign that he even noticed they were there.

Pink Anderson. Spartanburg, 1962.

Overleaf: *Pink Anderson teaching his son to play the guitar. Spartanburg, 1962.*

Gus Cannon

By the time the blues got on record most of the black musicians had given their banjos to their white neighbors, who had learned how to play by listening to what the black singers did with them. Gus was older than most of the other bluesmen, and he'd toured with medicine shows before World War I as "Banjo Joe," so he stayed faithful to his old instrument. He led the fine blues group Cannon's Jug Stompers that recorded for Victor Records in the 1920s, and one of their songs, "Walk Right In," became the number one pop single in the United States in a version by the Rooftop Singers in 1962. Gus wasn't flustered by all the excitement. When he listened back to himself in an interview I'd recorded with him in 1956, his response was an emphatic nod and the loud comment, "That's right!" and he picked up his banjo and played along with the song that came next on the record.

Cannon—which was what most of the musicians who knew him in Memphis called him— had tried his hand at growing cotton in some of the most repressive areas of the South before he began playing his banjo for a living, and to be sure that he never made a mistake in the way he addressed a white person he always called me "White Folk." In one of his recordings from the 1920s, however, he sang one of the handful of verses from that period that comment, even slyly, about the racial situation. In the first verse of the song "Feather Bed," he sang,

> *I remember the time just 'fore the war,*
> *Black man was sleepin' on shucks and straw.*
> *Now, praise God, old massa's dead,*
> *Black man sleepin' on a feather bed.*

*Gus Cannon.
Memphis, 1962.*

Henry Townsend

Henry Townsend was only a teenager when he recorded four blues for Columbia Records in 1929, and when I met him thirty-two years later he had a settled life as an insurance salesman in St. Louis. He hadn't played often over the years, but he had made the switch to electric guitar for his occasional jobs at local clubs. He still sang the way he had when he was younger, and there was considerable country blues feeling to his style. He had played for several years in the 1930s with an older St. Louis bluesman named Henry Spaulding. One of Spaulding's finest songs was called "Cairo Blues" named for the town in southern Illinois—and the accompaniment he played for it was different from anything anybody else was playing. When Spaulding had a chance to record in 1929, this was one of the songs he performed.

In 1961, while Henry and I were rehearsing for a new recording session, I asked him if he knew any old blues, and without hesitating he smiled and began to play the accompaniment for Spaulding's "Cairo Blues." He played and sang it just the way the older musician had done, in his own quiet way expressing the continuity of the blues traditions.

Henry Townsend.
St. Louis, 1962.

Lightning Hopkins

Lightning Hopkins was loose and disorganized and sometimes as impossible to deal with as an irritated mule, but he was also one of the greatest singers the blues has ever known. He was a compelling, emotional singer who could make up a blues about almost anything, and at the same time, with a disconcerting casualness, improvise an accompaniment to it with a way of playing the guitar that combined technical brilliance with an unforgettable dramatic intensity. He only needed three or four notes to catch his audience's attention.

When I found him in the Houston ghetto in 1959 his early career, doing singles for the R & B market, had been over for several years, and he was scuffling along Dowling Street, getting by as much on small scams and an occasional lucky day of gambling as he was by playing the blues. His electric guitar was in pawn, but the album we did with a rented acoustic in his barren bedroom in a rundown Houston rooming house caused such a sensation when it was released that within a few months he was one of the most popular "folk" blues artists performing for the blues revival audiences.

The last time I saw him, in 1975, we sat and talked out in front of his apartment in Houston. It was late afternoon, at the end of a long, hot Texas spring day. His new Buick was parked across the street from his wife's new Buick. We each had a can of beer in a sweating paper bag and we were watching the line of bumper to bumper traffic edging its way along the freeway not far from the street where he lived. Lightning, who had never worried much about getting anywhere, shrugged and gestured with his can of beer. "It take a lot out of a man to sit caught like that every day. Never could do it myself."

Sam "Lightning" Hopkins.
Houston, 1975.

A bluesman's hand. Daddy Hotcakes.

Revival Days

Revival Days

THE 1964 NEWPORT FOLK FESTIVAL AND THE BLUES REVIVAL

B Y THE EARLY 1960s so many people wanted to hear the old singers who had recently been rediscovered and who were still willing to perform that there was a new excitement over the country blues. It was described as a "revival," but since the blues had spent so much of its early years completely out of sight and hearing of the white audience it was in every sense a real discovery. Instead of performing occasionally for neighbors in their small southern towns or in the ghettos of the northern cities, the veteran blues artists found themselves singing for a new, young audience that didn't understand what they were doing very well, but made up for it by their enthusiasm and friendliness. It's obvious from the guarded expressions on the faces of most of the singers that they didn't understand much about what was happening to them either. Despite the misunderstanding, the blues became one of the strongest threads that was woven into the fabric of the '60s.

Perhaps the high point of the revival was the afternoon blues workshop at the Newport Folk Festival in 1964. The only one of the major rediscoveries who didn't perform was Son House, who wasn't able to get there in time. Skip James, one of the most enigmatic and startling of the Mississippi singers, came from a hospital in Belzonia, and his appearance on the stage marked the first time he had ever sung for a white audience.

The revival, however, touched much more widely than the stages at Newport. Sometimes we met the singers in Greenwich Village walk-ups, where they had a place to stay while they recorded or worked in the local clubs. Sometimes we met them on the streets or in the Village in front of the Folklore Center on Macdougal Street. Every city had its coffee house or its folk club where they performed. Through all of the confusion most of them

Preceding page:
Yank Rachel,
Sleepy John
Estes, and
Hammie Nixon.
Newport, 1964.

Above: *Reverend Robert Wilkins.*
Newport, 1964.

kept a wry, careful detachment that made it possible for them to deal with almost anything that happened.

Sometimes there were still reminders of what they'd gone through when they were younger. I was recording Big Joe Williams in a modern, beautifully decorated studio in Stockholm, Sweden, in 1974, and Joe had to get something out of his pocket to show me. He had spent a lot of time in the levee camps along the Mississippi River when he was just beginning to sing the blues, and he knew about keeping his papers and his money safe. He was wearing new slacks, but he had carefully made a small hole at the edge of one of the side pockets of the trousers. All of his papers were jammed into the single pocket, and he had closed it with a padlock.

Mississippi John Hurt and Skip James at the Newport Folk Festival, 1964.

Robert Pete Williams

". . . I come to the bar and there was these two fellows there, one with his head back, leanin', and the other one, a big man, and I was standin' there and he says, 'Where you from?' and I say 'Zachary,' and he says, 'You lyin','" and I says, 'No, I'm from Zachary,' and I got myself a quart of beer and I went over to the table with it to drink there with some boys I knew and after a moment the big one comes after me again, sayin' something, and I gets up and he says to the one leanin', 'I'm goin' take care of this . . .' and grabs my arm, grabs the sleeve, and I pulls away. I'm just small, and I don't want to fight him. I could of got away but the door done got blocked, you know, all the people who'd come up around to see like they do in a fight. He had a knife, a duckbill kind of knife with a broad blade and he come at me.

"I had the gun. That's the truth. I did have it. But Scotlandville's a bad place. They got men that won't stop at anything they's doin'. If I was to go there today I'd carry a gun. So he come at me and I shot him. In the stomach. But you know, he didn't go down, and it was a .45 I shot him with. He just stumbled a little and leaned on a table, then he started to come at me again.

"You know if you hit a man with a .45 and he don't go down he's strong—so I shot him again in the heart . . ."

For the shooting in the bar in Scotlandville in 1956 Robert Pete Williams was sentenced to life imprisonment at the Louisiana State work farm at Angola. Dr. Harry Oster, who was in the English Department at Louisiana State University in Baton Rouge, found him there in 1959 when he was collecting prison work songs, recorded his blues songs, and worked to get him released. Robert Pete was paroled in December of the same year, but he was sent to a white farmer to work out more years of his sentence as an indentured field hand. In 1964— in time for the Newport Folk Festival—he was finally free, and his smile on those gray, crowded Newport days shone with his feelings that somehow, in a way he still couldn't quite believe, his life was beginning again.

Robert Pete Williams at the Newport Folk Festival, 1964.

Mississippi John Hurt

John, more than any other of the singers from the early years of the blues, personified the revival of interest in the 1960s. He was a sweet, gentle, kind man with a sly humor and a completely unaffected response to everything that happened around him. He accompanied his sensitive blues ballads with a unique and complicated guitar technique that hadn't changed at all since he first recorded in 1928. After his appearances at Newport there was a flurry of instruction books and guitar teachers and correspondence lessons that tried as best they could to show new generations of young guitarists how to do what John did so naturally that he never thought about it. One of the most poignant tributes to him is the song "John Hurt," by folk singer Tom Paxton, which captures his quiet modesty in its guitar accompaniment which Tom plays in John's distinctive Mississippi finger-picking style.

John's story was one of the legends of the blues revival. He spent his life on a small farm in Mississippi, and except for his recording sessions in 1928 there was nothing to set him apart from his neighbors. The recordings were forgotten until two of the songs were included on the famous *Anthology of American Folk Music* on Folkways Records in 1952. When the book *The Country Blues* showed young blues enthusiasts that many of the old blues artists were still living and playing, there was an effort everywhere in the South to find as many of the blues veterans as possible. Hurt had never played professionally, so it seemed that he might never be found, but one of the songs he recorded was titled "Avalon Blues," and on a hunch that the Avalon of the title might be the small town of Avalon, Mississippi, in 1963 a researcher sent a letter to John c/o the postmaster in Avalon. A few weeks later I rang a doorbell at the quiet suburban home of blues collector Dick Spottswood outside of Washington, DC, and the door was answered by his guest, Mississippi John Hurt.

For the crowds at Newport there was always the memorable moment in John's set when he played his "Coffee Blues." At the end of the piece he reached under his chair and pulled out a Maxwell House coffee can which he held up for everyone to see, and then assured us, with mock seriousness, "It's good to the last drop."

Mississippi John Hurt at the Newport Folk Festival, 1964.

Skip James

Skip James was one of the most enigmatic and complicated of all the Mississippi blues artists and it was almost impossible to believe that a group of young enthusiasts had found him in a hospital in Belzonia and that they were bringing him up to Newport for the blues workshop in 1964. When I introduced him I could tell that he'd been sick and he was still weak, and I wasn't sure he'd be able to perform. But with the first line of his blues there was the unmistakable falsetto voice and the subtly intricate guitar accompaniment that had set an indelible mark on his first recordings. He soon became a regular performer on the circuit of small coffee houses and clubs where the revival flourished, and he became even better known later in the 1960s when the group Cream recorded his song "I'm So Glad."

When Ann photographed him in Greenwich Village after the festival he'd been away from Mississippi for only a few weeks, and he was looking as curiously at her as she was at him.

Skip James.
New York, 1964.

Son House

Son grew up in northern Mississippi playing with the singer Charlie Patton, who probably comes as close as we'll ever get to a "father" of the blues, and the handful of recordings Son made at the end of the 1920's are among the most sought after blues collectors items. When he was playing for little Saturday night cabin dances outside of Robinsonville, Mississippi, his "apprentice" was a very young Robert Johnson, who has become the most legendary blues artist of them all. The musical progression went from Patton and Son House to Robert Johnson, and from Johnson to Muddy Waters, Howling Wolf, and Elmore James, and from Muddy and Elmore to the Rolling Stones, Eric Clapton, and so much of the rock of the 1960s. Son had left the South during World War II, but a group of young researchers finally tracked him down in Rochester, New York, and he went on to have a long and successful second career. He hadn't performed since the 1940s, so his guitar playing had lost some of its fire, but he still played in the same style, and his singing was as fiercely emotional as it had been when he'd made his first recordings. Sometimes when he was singing you had the feeling that if you closed your eyes you could be out on a back porch on a hot night with Son and Charlie and "little" Robert, and you were there at the genesis of all the music you'd ever heard.

Son House back-stage at Carnegie Hall. New York, 1965.

Memphis Willie B., Furry Lewis, and Gus Cannon

Sometimes the country blues singers were brought up from the South by people who were running the major festivals and concerts, but just as often it was somebody from the new young blues audience. The "promoters" didn't have much money, but they knew who they wanted to hear, and often they were responsible for some of the most unexpected concerts. A group called The Friends of Old Time Music was sponsoring a series of concerts at a small theater on the NYU campus in Greenwich Village, and they brought up three of the Memphis singers to perform some of their blues and also to play together as a jug band, the way they had in Memphis in the 1920s. Cannon, of course, had been the leader of his Jug Stompers, while Furry and Willie B. usually worked as bluesmen, but it was clear, once they began playing and clowning on the stage together, that all three of them had been part of the golden days along Beale Street.

There wasn't much money for the trip, so they came up together sitting in the back of a Greyhound bus, sharing a cardboard box filled with chicken and cake that Willie B.'s wife had packed for them. She had packed so much food that they still had half of the cake left when we met them at the bus depot.

New York was a series of surprises for them, but they were as much of a surprise to the people they met. A half an hour before they stood on the steps of the Folklore Center to get

Memphis Willie B., Furry Lewis, and Gus Cannon at The Folklore Center in Greenwich Village. New York, 1965.

their picture taken they had been talking to Izzy Young, who owned the store inside. While we were standing around Izzy's little shop a young white guitar player who looked like he was still in college brought in a girl he wanted to impress. He was so busy with her that he didn't notice any of the rest of us, including Furry, who was leaning against a rack of LPs. The boy picked up one of the guitars that was always sitting on a back counter and told the girl he was going to show her how Furry Lewis played "John Henry." He got through two or three choruses, then looked up when he realized that somebody was standing in front of him.

Keeping a straight face, Furry took the guitar out of the boy's hands and began finger-picking "John Henry," adding some embellishments that I'd never heard him play before. He finished with a rhythmic tag that he rapped out on the guitar with his knuckles, did a little buck and wing dance step, and at the same time with his other hand pushed his hat down over his eyes. The boy was too flabbergasted to say anything, and Furry casually turned around and went on with what he'd been telling us, pretending that he didn't want to smile.

Sometimes the older musicians had lost some of their finger dexterity, and their voices had gotten rough and coarse, but being able to hear them at all brought the country blues traditions to life again. It wasn't only that now we could watch their fingers to see how they played that strum or that rhythm figure: they knew songs that they'd never had a chance to record, and they could tell us about the singer over on the next cotton plantation who never got to make a record at all, or about the old man in the cabin close by the levee who taught them their first chords. For everyone, the singers and those of us who were fortunate enough to hear them, there was a poignant sense that this was a moment that would never happen again.

Chicago

Chicago

THE URBAN BLUES

THE BLACK MIGRATION out of the South, which had already begun surreptitiously before the Civil War, increased steadily in the decades that followed, and with the opening of the factory jobs in the northern cities during World War I it became a flood that changed the social texture of life in America. The L&N Railroad went through the heart of Mississippi north to Chicago, and despite bloody efforts by the plantation owners to hold their laborers on the land with a surge of lynchings in Mississippi and Tennessee, thousands of blacks managed to escape. Once in Chicago, they soon found jobs in the city's growing industries.

Most of the newcomers moved to the South Side of the city, close to the busy stockyards, which always had some kind of job opening. Further south, along the lake, close to the border with Indiana, there were steel mills. As the African American community grew it spread to most of the South Side, and then into the West Side. What was happening in Chicago was one current of the broad stream that was bringing people from the Atlantic states north to Harlem, and people from all of the southern states to other northern cities like Cleveland and Detroit.

The same railroad that passed through Mississippi began its journey in New Orleans, so jazz was one of the first things that made its way to the new neighborhoods. The blues made the trip a few years later. The reasons were simple: the people streaming into the northern cities were lonely. Many of them were young men who had made the trips by themselves, and they were hungry to hear the music they'd grown up with. Chicago soon was filled with clubs and cafes and dance halls and theaters, all of them featuring musicians from the southern states. The fancier places employed the jazz orchestras, and if you went out to dance in the 1920s you could shimmy to Louis Armstrong with King Oliver's Jazz Band at

Lincoln Gardens, or do the black bottom to Johnny Dodds and his New Orleans Wanderers at Kelly's Stables. Most of the legendary jazz artists of the 1920s, from Bix Beiderbecke and Benny Goodman to Jelly Roll Morton and Bessie Smith, worked somewhere in Chicago during these years.

The less pretentious cafes had the blues—first the singers who accompanied themselves with a guitar or piano, and then small groups that played as string bands or blues trios. With so many musicians in the city it soon became the center of a busy recording scene, and nearly every important blues artist recorded in Chicago at one time or another. Even though Chicago was a large city—at that time the second largest in the country—the black society that had established itself in the city was still close to its country roots.

It was a blues musician who didn't make it to Chicago to record, Robert Johnson, who was the dominant influence on the blues that emerged there after World War II. A young Mississippi field hand named McKinley Morganfield listened to Johnson's records from the 1930s and with a new name, Muddy Waters, he developed a guitar style based on Johnson's that was also beautifully suited to the new electric guitars that were making their way into the South Side blues clubs. Another South Side singer, Elmore James, learned Johnson' technique with the slide and presented his own version of Johnson's music in a style that was as brilliantly inventive as the one Muddy Waters had developed.

New instruments began to appear in the clubs. A generation of young harmonica players learned to play their "Mississippi saxophones" with a microphone cupped against the back of the harmonica. The bands added drums and bass in the style of the popular rhythm-and-blues artists. By the 1950s the Chicago blues had become one of the most exciting musical styles in the country, and it was only a few years before their music was discovered by the young rock musicians who introduced it to the world.

Muddy Waters

In the late 1940s a young guitar player and singer named McKinley Morganfield, who had grown up on a plantation outside of Stovall, Mississippi, and recently migrated to Chicago, developed a new style of blues using an electric guitar and a rhythm accompaniment with some of the beat of the new R&B bands. He had a day job delivering venetian blinds, and at night he played around the South Side clubs with a small group of friends who understood what he was trying to do. One day in 1948, a pianist he had worked with named Sunnyland Slim, also from Mississippi, was able to arrange a recording session with a small company called Aristocrat Records, and he managed to locate Muddy, who was out in his truck making deliveries. Muddy called his boss, told him his cousin had been found dead in an alley, and hurried to the studio. He stayed with Aristocrat for the rest of the year, sometimes recording with Sunnyland, sometimes with just a bass player. By the next year he had expanded the group, and he recorded with a full rhythm section, a rhythm guitar back-up, and a harmonica player, Little Walter Jacobs. The new Chicago electric blues sound had been born.

Through the 1950s Muddy's "home club"—where he could be found when he wasn't on tour—was Pepper's Lounge, on the South Side. None of the recording stars like Muddy played the first set of the night. It was the band's chance to work on some of their own material and to get the crowd warmed up. Muddy, however, usually sat out both the first and second sets. He sat at a small table close to the bandstand, a figure of such immense dignity and presence that he filled the club even when he wasn't playing. The first night I saw him there in 1959 the band had a guest singer for the second set. B. B. King was in town, and he was up at the microphone beside Otis Spann, sweaty with the raw excitement of the music, and turning every now and then to look over and smile at Muddy, to let him know he hadn't forgotten whose club he was in.

Muddy Waters.
New York, 1965.

Otis Spann

Otis played the piano in Muddy Waters' band for so many years that his career is always associated with Muddy's, even though he also played and recorded with almost every blues artist in Chicago, from Howling Wolf to Bo Diddley. He was so close to Muddy and his wife that some people thought they were cousins but they were simply close friends. He was also from Mississippi, but he'd grown up in Jackson, the state capital, so he fit easily into the city environment of the South Side. He was soft-spoken and comfortable, and he was one of those rare musicians who can adapt immediately to any group they're playing with. He was in the rhythm section for an album I was recording with a very young Buddy Guy, and the imagination of his solos and the intensity of his accompaniments pushed Buddy to one of his best afternoons in the studio. In one of the slow blues there was a moment of hushed respect in Buddy's voice as he turned his head to tell Otis that he had the next solo: "Mr. Spann, if you please."

Otis Spann.
Chicago, 1965.

Otis Rush

When I auditioned Otis for the series *Chicago/The Blues/Today!* that I was producing for Vanguard Records in December 1965, he was leading a band that blended the blues and current R&B at a West Side Chicago club called Curley's. It was a large, dark, high ceilinged space close to the elevated tracks that had been turned into a music lounge. He was performing brilliantly, with the sting and the individual flair that had characterized his guitar work from the beginning of his career. In the studio a few days later he recorded a strong, blues-steeped set, and there was so much excitement over his contribution to the series that it seemed he would go on to have the kind of career that someone like Muddy Waters or B. B. King was enjoying. Instead, when he was approached for a solo album he couldn't decide whether he wanted to record again, he couldn't put new material together, and he was uncertain about plans to tour extensively and work enough to keep his band together. This moment, captured as he was standing outside the old RCA studio down by the lake front, was one of the bright stretches in a career that had its uneven patches of light and dark.

Otis Rush.
Chicago, 1965.

Little Walter

Little Walter (Walter Jacobs) was the first harmonica player with Muddy Water's band, and these recordings, along with his own releases with his band "Little Walter and the Jukes," defined the Chicago blues harp sound. He was also an alcoholic, and his career fell apart only a few years after he did his best known recordings. He was thirty-eight when he died in 1968. By the mid-1960s he was working only sporadically, and it was usually when a friend like guitarist Lee Jackson came and brought him to the club. I wanted to include him in the Vanguard series, but he was too nervous to come to the studio. When Ann photographed him he was waiting for Lee's band to finish its warm-up set, and he seemed almost apprehensive as he looked up at Lee and waited for the moment when he had to stand up and take over the band.

Little Walter waiting to play with
Lee Jackson's band. Chicago, 1965.

Sweet Home Chicago . . .

J. B. HUTTO and his HAWKS playing at the Blue Lounge, 1965.

The Blue Lounge was a rough club under the elevated tracks on Indiana Avenue. Walter Horton, the harmonica player, offered to take us, since he thought it wasn't a good idea for us to go by ourselves. We met Walter in the battered tenement where he lived behind a door scarred with innumerable locks, down hallways glaring with dangling bare bulbs. We stayed with the band until a neighborhood bully began making insistent advances toward the drummer's young wife. When we went outside into the snowy darkness a police car was across the street, waiting to see that nothing happened to us. Walter was attacked and stabbed when he walked back to his apartment an hour later.

J. B. Hutto

Hutto was a second-generation blues man who had picked up his bottleneck style from watching Muddy Waters and Elmore James playing around the South Side. He was one of the few Chicago artists who wasn't from Mississippi—he was born in South Carolina—but after a few years of hearing their music he picked up some of their hard-eyed insistence. He was so quiet and unassuming in the recording studio that the harsh power of his blues always stung with surprise for the first few bars of a new piece.

J. B. Hutto.
Chicago, 1965.

Shakey Walter Horton

Other musicians usually thought of Walter as the best harp player on the South Side, and his recordings with Muddy when Little Walter wasn't with the band had been an important influence on everybody who started playing later. He could be moody and unpredictable, and when he was in the studio there was no way of knowing what would happen until the band started recording. He was tall and battered, and his life was as unpredictable as his playing, but he was always willing to work with younger players. On the Vanguard series he even recorded a duet with the young Charlie Musselwhite, who was shifting from the acoustical harmonica he'd learned to play in Memphis to the "Mississippi saxophone," as the electrified harmonica was called in the South Side clubs.

Shakey Walter Horton with (left) bluesman Johnny Young. Chicago, 1965.

Johnny Shines

Shines had made a handful of startling records for a small Chicago record company in the early 1950s, then he had dropped out of sight. When he was rediscovered two or three months before the Vanguard sessions it turned out that he had been working in the South Side blues clubs for several years—but as a photographer, not a musician. It was particularly exciting to talk to him, because he was one of the few Chicago musicians who had met Robert Johnson and traveled with him when they both were still living in the South. The first night I met Johnny—with Walter Horton sitting across the table from us in Johnny's apartment—we sat up long into the night with a fifth of Teacher's while he and Walter talked about the blues, about the South they'd managed to leave behind them, and about Robert Johnson. The first song Johnny did in the studio was his reworking of one of Robert's pieces, played with a slide, and he came as close to Johnson's haunted, raw emotionalism as anyone I'd ever recorded.

Johnny Shines.
Chicago, 1965

Willie Dixon

For Willie, coming down to the RCA studios on the lakefront for the Vanguard session was like coming home, since he'd begun his career recording there for RCA's Bluebird series in the old days of 78 rpm singles. Although he was another Mississippian—he was born in Vicksburg, on the banks of the river—he didn't turn to the blues until Muddy Waters' breakthrough with the Chicago electric blues style in the late 1940s. As a boy he sang in gospel groups and learned to play the bass; then when he moved to Chicago in 1935 he became a heavyweight boxer. It wasn't until 1940 that he began to utilize his musical skills, and his first Bluebird sessions were with a "jive" group called The Five Breezes. After The Five Breezes there was a group called The Four Jumps of Jive, then he had his biggest pre-blues success with the trio The Big Three, that recorded for Columbia in 1946 and 1947. He played his big acoustic bass and sang harmonies.

At the beginning of the 1950s, as R&B was fading, and the first rush of excitement over the Chicago blues began, Dixon worked first as a producer for Cobra Records, a small local label that had Otis Rush as one of its artists, then became an Artist and Repertory director for Chess, the premier Chicago blues label. In 1954 he began his career as a song writer, when he composed his first piece for Muddy Waters, and he turned himself into one of the most prolific and successful commercial blues writers. His "Hoochie Coochie Man" became a standard, but he had innumerable hits, such as "I Can't Quit You Baby" with Otis Rush and "I'm Ready" with Muddy Waters.

When Willie came to the studio to play on the Homesick James session he was as interested in song writing as he was in playing the bass. He fell in with the friendly mood of the sessions, and stayed to talk with the other musicians waiting to record. During a break in the Junior Wells session I heard an earnest, soft voiced murmuring from the couch in the control room. Dixon had just composed a new blues and he was trying to teach it to Junior in time for him to go out in the studio and put it on record. Junior was thinking of a dozen other things, but this was Willie Dixon so he tried to listen but he finally shook his head with a grin. He couldn't get a new song that fast! Willie shrugged cheerfully, and looked around for somebody else who might want to sing his latest blues.

Sunnyland Slim and Homesick James

Homesick, the man on the right, hadn't had as many chances to record in the 1950s, and for him the Vanguard sessions were an important chance to become a little better known. His expression was relaxed and easy, since we'd just finished with his band. Sunnyland Slim, the taller man on the left, had recorded so often since his first session with Muddy Waters in the late 1940s that it seemed more important to let some of the lesser known musicians have a chance. He dropped by the studio anyway, ostensibly to see his friends, but his expression suggests his hope that he might be asked to sit down at the piano and play a song or two.

"Sunnyland Slim" (Albert Luandrew)
and "Homesick" James Williamson.
Chicago, 1965.

Buddy Guy

When I asked Buddy to sign an exclusive artist's contract with Vanguard in 1967, he was playing two or three nights a week with Junior Wells in Theresa's, a friendly, rundown basement club at 48th and Indiana, and working days repairing cars. His wife didn't want him to play more often than that, knowing what the life of a touring musician would do to their family. But the blues meant too much for him to give up his chance to have a career, and he'd already gotten so much attention for the albums he'd recorded with Junior that there was no way for him to stay on the South Side. Except for brief periods, after he opened his own blues club in Chicago, he was steadily out on the road.

Sometimes, watching him play in the 1960s could be a surprising experience. Instead of playing small clubs like Theresa's he found himself playing in places like the Fillmore Auditorium in San Franciso, before the shows were moved to a hall that had seats. At the old Fillmore the bands played for crowds that stretched out in front of the bandstand, or drew pictures on the floor under the glo-lights hanging from some of the pillars, or looked around the walls at the light show—and sometimes even danced. Buddy was used to the shows at the big theaters on the South Side where one of the most popular parts of the evening was a number where the featured artist went down into the crowd in the front rows. At a show in one of the theaters I saw Major Lance, who had a hit record at that moment, go down into the waiting crowd and then have to claw his way back to the stage, with the ushers helping him by swinging their flashlights at people, his clothes half torn off, his hair tangled, and a shoe gone. He finished the show in a bathrobe.

One night when I was watching Buddy at the Fillmore he jumped down off the stage to do his variation of the old theater routine. His specialty was to go out into the crowd playing his guitar, while the band on the stage kept playing the riff behind him until he climbed back to join them. But for this show, since it was the Fillmore and the crowd was so laid back, when he got to the end of the long guitar cord that plugged him back in to the

Buddy Guy.
Chicago, 1965.

amplifier on stage, he handed the guitar to three or four people who were sitting in the middle of the dance floor. Instead of playing he kept on through the crowd singing his blues over and over while the band kept pumping out the chords for him on stage. I stayed close to him, curious to see what would happen. He went on singing and working his way through the entire building. The band's sound was a little thin when he got downstairs to the lobby, and people who didn't know what was happening jumped out of his way, obviously shaken by the sudden appearance of a man in a flapping suit and sweat-soaked shirt and tie who kept shouting the same blues verse over and over. There was another tense moment when he burst into the men's toilet, still singing, and interrupted a drug buy that was going on in a corner.

About halfway through the haphazard tour of the building, I became aware that there was a guitar playing a crackling blues lead along with the band. When Buddy finally got back to the dance floor, a little hoarse by now and wringing wet with perspiration, most of the crowd had gathered around the group in the middle of the floor where he had dropped his guitar. Without noticing what he was doing, Buddy had handed it to Elvin Bishop, guitarist with the Paul Butterfield Blues Band. After a few choruses Elvin started to play, and now Buddy couldn't get through the crowd to get the guitar back. He circled the crowd two or three times, singing with a little less enthusiasm, and finally he had to go back onstage and sing a final chorus with his band, who by this point were as wringing wet and ragged as he was. When he caught his breath he had to ask nervously for whoever was playing his guitar to please bring it back to him.

Otis Spann.
Chicago, 1965.

Junior Wells,
singing at
Theresa's Club.
Chicago, 1967

Junior Wells and Buddy Guy at Theresa's.

Shakey Walter Horton's Harmonicas

*In the studio for
Chicago/The Blues/Today!,
1965*

Elga Edmond's borrowed drums

Chicago, 1965

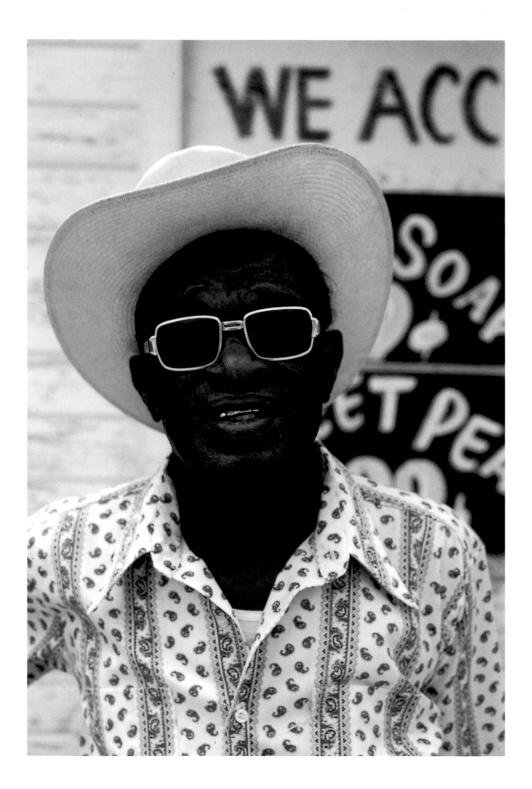

Lightning Hopkins.
Houston, 1974.

Clifton Chenier,
Lafayette, 1983

*Rocking Dopsie at
the New Orleans
Jazz Festival, 1984.*

Zydeco!

LOUISIANA's JUMP-UP BLUES

ZYDECO MUSIC—western Louisiana's way of playing the blues—has all the feel of an old folk music style, but it first began to develop in the 1950s, and zydeco today is continuing to change and shift as new instruments make their way into the bands, along with a fresh array of songs and rhythms. That part of Louisiana was settled by French refugees from "Acadia," the island off the Canadian coast that was renamed Nova Scotia after its capture by the British in 1755. A distinctive musical style emerged around the "Cajun" French dialect and a repertory of waltzes and two-steps that go back several generations in the Cajun culture. Part of the unique sound of Cajun music was a little button accordion that German settlers brought into that part of the country after the Civil War. There were both black and white Cajun bands, and there was a unique black tradition of the French language and culture that was also different in other ways from the black culture of the rest of the South, since most of the black families in Louisiana were free. The French Acadians, perhaps because of their own unhappy experience as captives of the British, generally were not slave holders.

During World War II many people from the Louisiana French speaking areas drifted west to Houston to find work in the new war industries and they missed their own music, food, and dancing. By the 1950s some of the black musicians from Louisiana towns like Lafayette, Opelousas, and Lake Charles had begun playing regularly in little bars in the Houston ghetto. The music was still a mixture of Cajun melodies and half remembered R & B hits, but already the new style was beginning to emerge. The first instrument to change was the accordion. In Louisiana most of the bands stayed with the old square, button instrument, with its two scales and limited harmonic possibilities, but some of the younger musicians, led by Lafayette's Clifton Chenier, began playing a more modern keyboard accordion, with its bluesier sound.

Despite the cultural isolation and the poverty in the Cajun areas of Louisiana there was no way to keep the music isolated, and the new Chicago electric blues and modern R&B were becoming increasingly popular. Zydeco was a blend of the old French traditions, along with everything else that was streaming in over the radio and the juke boxes. The name came from one of the first songs played by the new bands. In the beginning it was only an over-and-over melodic figure played on the accordion and the washboard, since it had no harmonic structure. Most of the bands still play the piece the same way today, adding a repetitive bass part and a saxophone riff. It is clearly of African origin, and the sound of the melody has given zydeco its distinctive character. The original piece was usually known as "Les Haricots Ne Pas Salé," which translates as something like "the snap beans aren't salty." Since it was that piece that identified the new style the name for the music soon became a corrupted version of the song title, "Les Haricots," which in the local French dialect becomes "lezarico," and which was then bastardized into "zydeco." "Zydeco," however, is only one of the west Louisiana spellings for the style. You might drive past a dance hall out in the country and see a poster advertising "Zordico" music, and on an early recording by Lightning Hopkins, when the Houston bluesman was experimenting with the new sound, it was called "zologo" music.

The washboard has continued to be a distinctive part of the zydeco sound, as the first groups were usually little two- or three-piece ensembles that couldn't find a way to work a full drum set or a bass into their melodies. However, it has since progressed from a humble laundry accessory to a commercially made ribbed vest constructed out of sheet metal and hung over the shoulders. The new name for it is the "frottoir." Cleveland Chenier played the frottoir in his brother Clifton's band, scraping out the rhythms with a metal beer bottle opener.

In the early years there was no question that Chenier was the "King of Zydeco," and he occasionally wore an elaborate crown when he played for a local dance. He added instruments to his band—bass and saxophone—and the instrumental sound he developed with his Red Hot Louisiana Band, as well as the compositions he wrote and arranged, are the bedrock of the zydeco style. When his lifetime struggle against diabetes left him too sick to tour steadily in the 1970s there was a heated competition among the other Louisiana accordion players to take over his crown. So many other musicians began calling themselves the "King of Zydeco" that the recording engineer Mark Miller, who was doing most of the zydeco recording in his studio in Crowley, a small town not far from Lafayette, threatened to start wearing a crown when he was sitting in the control room: "You all calling yourself 'Kings of Zydeco.' I might as well get a crown for myself!"

Cleveland Chenier.
Lafayette, 1982.

Clifton Chenier

Clifton was a proud, commanding man who spent most of his life playing his accordion in dance halls in western Louisiana and west Texas, keeping an excellent band together and composing many of the pieces that are now zydeco standards. Part of his success was also due to his fortuitous meeting with Chris Strachwitz, a young blues enthusiast who owned his own record label, Arhoolie Records. Chris met Clifton on one of his trips to the South and realized that he could give Clifton the opportunity to record as much and as often as he liked, and through the Arhoolie distribution to the folk blues audience he could spread Clifton's music to a broader audience. Strachwitz also quickly discovered that large numbers of Louisiana people had moved to the Oakland and Richmond areas in California, and they were hungry for some of Clifton's down home music. For several years the band appeared in the California zydeco and folk clubs. Strachwitz also released singles that he promoted in Clifton's home territory, so the band was still as well known in Louisiana as they were in the rest of country.

In his years of illness, Chenier found his record sales slipping, and he quarreled with Strachwitz. Crippled with diabetes, he paid his medical bills by borrowing money from friends, organizing benefit dances, and holding "barbecue breakfasts" at his home in Lafayette, where his wife sold sandwiches from the kitchen window.

It became harder and harder for him to pull open the bellows on a standard accordion, so he moved to a newer instrument with an electronic keyboard and a smaller bellows. The sound was different from his acoustic instrument, but it made it possible for him to continue playing. The change didn't effect his musical creativity or the band's energy. The album we did together, *I'm Here,* won a Grammy Award in 1983.

Clifton Chenier playing at the Blue Flame Lounge. Lafayette, 1982.

Rocking Dopsie

Whatever arguments there may have been over who followed Clifton Chenier as the "King of Zydeco," Dopsie—whose name is pronounced "Doopsie"—was crowned king by the mayor of Lafayette, and he sometimes wore a crown on stage, just as Clifton used to do. As Alton Rubin, his real name, he grew up on a farm outside of Lafayette and the hard times of the Depression forced him to give up school and work in the fields when he was thirteen. One day he picked up his brother's accordion to try it out, but since he's left handed he picked it up upside down. He played it that way for the rest of his life, teaching himself the keyboard with the treble keys on the bottom. He used his right hand to accent the rhythm with the chord buttons normally used for harmony.

None of this stopped Dopsie from being one of the most colorful and exuberant of the zydeco performers. He worked so hard on the bandstand that once when he walked off the stage after a set I saw he was leaving foot prints with the sweat coming through the soles of his shoes. I produced Dopsie's albums for a Swedish record company, and we flew the band over on a summer weekend for the company's 25th anniversary party. One night they played for a moonlight steamer excursion through the islands off the Swedish coast, and as they started their first set small boats began drifting toward us and people called out, "Who's that playing?" We shouted back that it was Rocking Dopsie and his Cajun Twisters, and most of the boats stayed alongside for a moment. Dopsie and the band were playing in an open space between decks, and the dancers were visible along the railings. About midnight I went up on the top deck and looked back and there was a fleet of boats following us in the moonlight, people crowded on the narrow decks to listen in wonder to Dopsie and his music.

Rocking Dopsie.
Houston, 1983.

Morris Ardoin

The Ardoin family all took their turns in the family orchestra, which accompanied their father, the legendary accordion player "Boi-Sec" Ardoin. Their little band—often with Kenry Fontenot on fiddle—was the most traditional of the local bands, and they all had to work day jobs to support their music. Morris, who was the most business-like of the family and usually ran the orchestra, had been injured on the job a few days before we were to record an album in the old Miller Studio in Crowley.

Morris Ardoin.
Crowley,
Louisiana, 1975.

Kenry Fontenot

Kenry was one of the last of the great fiddlers who helped shape black French music. He worked hard on a farm close to his home in Welch, Louisiana, and sometimes he didn't feel like playing, but when he showed up for a festival or an occasional job with the Ardoin brothers his fiddle style seemed to come surging out of some forgotten moment in time before there was even a word "blues." Once after we'd been rehearsing late on a hot night at Lawrence Ardoin's house I asked Kenry about the years when he'd stopped playing, and what had gotten him started again. He shook his head.

"I forgot about music for a while, but Clifton Chenier will talk to you when he's broke, and he talked to me in a club in Lawtell. And he asked me, 'You still playin' a violin?' and I said, 'Only now and then. I've most give up music.' And he said, 'Give up your wife, give up your family, but don't give up your music. Me, I'm the best on accordion there is, and you the best fiddler in Louisiana. You can't give it up. If you work with your hands you'll always stay low, but with music you can rise up most to the top. I've been to most every country there is, just because of my music, and it could happen to you . . .'"

Kenry Fontenot.
Lafayette, 1972.

Chester Zeno, frottoir (washboard), with Rocking Dopsie's Cajun Twisters. Chester was already playing with Dopsie for tips in local bars when they started off together as teenagers as an accordion-washboard duet. Houston, 1983.

John Hart, with the Cajun Twisters. John was a mainstay of Clifton Chenier's band for several years, but when Clifton began traveling less John came into Dopsie's band for a recording session, and he stayed for several years. His name was misspelled "Hoyt" on the piece Dopsie played for Paul Simon's "Graceland" album.

Alton Rubin Jr., Dopsie's son, came into the band as a teenager for the same recording session when John Hart joined, and he's never left. Houston, 1983.

A Note on the Photos

The photographs from Africa, Louisiana, and Texas, the photographs in the introduction from New Orleans, Alabama, and Memphis, as well as the portraits of Pink Anderson (standing), Bukka White, and Lightning Hopkins are by Samuel Charters. All other photographs are by Ann Charters.

List of Books, Record Jackets, and Articles

WHERE THE PHOTOS FIRST APPEARED